Island Heritage

A Guided Tour to Lake Erie's Bass Islands

Island Heritage

A GUIDED TOUR TO
Lake Erie's Bass Islands

TED LIGIBEL and RICHARD WRIGHT

With a Foreword by
Charles E. Herdendorf

◆

Ohio State University Press
COLUMBUS

Historical photographs from Arthur F. Boyles Collection, Put-In-Bay, Ohio

Library of Congress Cataloging-in-Publication Data
Ligibel, Ted
    Island heritage.

    Includes index.
    1. Bass Islands (Ohio)—Description and travel—Tours.
2. Erie, Lake, Region—Description and travel—Tours. I. Wright, Richard J. II. Title.
F497.08L54   1987   917.7.1'2   87–5742
ISBN 0–8142–0442–2 (pbk.)

Dedication

Island Heritage is dedicated to the memory of Dr. Richard J. Wright whose untimely death in September 1986 left an unfillable void in the pursuit and dissemination of Great Lakes' history and lore. As the author of this book's section on the steamers and ferries so vital to Lake Erie's rich history, Rick Wright drew upon his years of experience and interest in maritime history. It was his personal archives that formed the basis for the Insititute for Great Lakes Research, the largest collection of Great Lakes' documents, photographs, and related material in the nation.

Dr. Wright's vast knowledge of the Great Lakes and of the people and the hundreds of vessels that have plied their waters earned him an international reputation.

It was an honor for me to collaborate on this work and to have been his associate at Bowling Green State University's Center for Archival Collections for several years. Dr. Wright's legacy will live on in this and dozens of other writings and in his Institute's collections, which will serve as the primary Great Lakes maritime heritage resource for generations to come.

Ted J. Ligibel

Contents

Foreword

Island Heritage originated nearly a decade ago when the Center for Archival Collections, an integral part of the Bowling Green State University, and the Historic Preservation Office for Northwest Ohio collaborated to conduct a survey of historic structures on the Bass Islands in western Lake Erie. This survey, sponsored by a grant from the Ohio Department of Natural Resources, identified and inventoried over two hundred island buildings.

At that time, the Center for Archival Collection had the largest documentary holding in the country dealing with Great Lakes maritime history and the Lake Erie islands region. Of particular importance was the Center's extensive historical information and photographs of the many ships (a few are included in this book) that were identified with servicing the islands during the past one hundred thirty years. Recently these collections were moved to a new facility in Perrysburg, Ohio, where Bowling Green State University founded the Institute for Great Lakes Research.

In 1980, based on their previous experience, Dr. Richard J. Wright, the Center's director, and Mr. Theodore J. Ligibel, historic preservation officer for northwest Ohio, proposed to the Ohio Sea Grant Program that a project be sponsored to prepare a publication entitled "Portrait of the Bass Islands: A Handbook of Architecture and History." They argued that no definitive handbook existed which detailed the unique historical environment of the Bass Islands on the western end of Lake Erie. The principal objective of their project was to produce a high quality booklet that put together two factors—structures and ships—to bring out the unique heritage of the islands. Interrelated with the island traditions and the isolation imposed by the geographical conditions of the nineteenth century are maritime activities. This dependency upon water transportation for both passenger and freight has intensified the nostalgia of the island heritage.

Dr. Wright and Mr. Ligibel were successful in their proposal and in September 1981, supported by an Ohio Sea Grant award, began work on *Island Heritage*. Funding came from the Ohio Sea Grant Program, the National Sea Grant College Program, the National Oceanic and Atmospheric Administration, the U.S. Department of Commerce (grant number NA81AA-D-00095, project A/P-2), and from the State of Ohio.

Many islanders contributed to the work, particularly Jeff Koehler, local historian, and Mary Beckford, reporter with the Port Clinton *News Herald*. Harry Myers, superintendent of Perry's Victory and International Peace Memorial, National Park Service, graciously supplied many historical photographs from the Herbster Collection. The staff at the Center for Archival Collections worked hard to see that both authors were able to produce this work. Maps were illustrated by Sue Abbati of the Ohio Sea Grant Program. Editorial work was done by Kay Ward Davis and Sarah Serafim. Preproduction coordination was provided by Maran Brainard of the Ohio Sea Grant Program.

Dr. Wright's untimely passing in September 1986 has left a tremendous void in the ranks of Great Lakes maritime scholars. His accomplishments in this field are many and we are pleased to be able to publish this, his final work. Ted Ligibel currently serves as Historic Resources Planner for the Urban Affairs Center at the University of Toledo.

CHARLES E. HERDENDORF, DIRECTOR
Center for Lake Erie Area Research
Ohio Sea Grant Program
Franz Theodore Stone Laboratory
The Ohio State University

Put-in-Bay, Ohio
January 14, 1987

Preface

Located in western Lake Erie and easily accessible by ferry from the mainland, Ohio's Bass Islands—South Bass, Middle Bass, North Bass, and Gibraltar—feature an exciting variety of sights and activities for tourists. Grand old summer homes, quaint public buildings, wineries and ancient stone wine cellars, picturesque farmhouses, and unique caves are but a few of the scenic and historical attractions found scattered throughout these isles.

This guidebook is intended to give to the Bass Islands tourist an accurate and informative description of the area and its places of interest. Eight tours of varying lengths are found in these pages. Each tour can be completed in a few hours or less, and detailed explanations are given about the stopping points.

Numbered maps pinpointing the sights on each tour are also included, as are many photographs that depict buildings no longer present or identify architectural styles. A history of the island steamship trade and photographs of some of the steamships follow the tours. The glossary of architectural styles and terms is designed to help the beginner identify and appreciate the various architectural styles found in the islands.

We hope that, in addition to increasing the tourist's enjoyment of the Bass Islands, this guidebook will serve as a souvenir and will evoke many pleasant memories of the region in the years to come.

Note
Many of the structures highlighted in
Island Heritage are privately owned.
Visitors should respect personal property rights.

Introduction to the Bass Islands

Little is known about the history of the Bass Islands prior to the 1800s. Scientists tell us that these and the neighboring land masses were formed by glaciers during the Ice Age; grooves left by the huge moving masses of ice can still be seen in some of the islands' limestone surfaces. Thousands of years later, members of several Indian tribes, including the Ottawa, Wyandot, Miami, and Delaware, frequented the islands, especially during the hunting season, when fish and fowl were abundant and fat raccoons were plentiful.

By 1700, the four islands of the Bass group—South Bass, Middle Bass, North Bass, and Gibraltar—had probably been sighted by the French-Canadian fur trader and explorer Louis Jolliet, who in 1669 was one of the first white men to sail on Lake Erie. Ten years later, in 1679, the French explorer René de la Salle may have landed at Middle Bass Island during one of his lake voyages, accompanied by another Frenchman, the explorer and missionary Father Louis Hennepin, who reportedly offered the first Catholic mass on Middle Bass and named the island Isle de Fleur, or Island of Flowers.

During the next hundred years, the island group was visited by numerous explorers, trappers, and military men. The islands were charted in the late 1700s by the British, who subsequently relinquished their claims as a result of the Revolutionary War. After the Revolution, the lands were designated as part of Connecticut's Western Reserve, and by 1795 the ownership of the islands had passed from the state of Connecticut to a group called the Connecticut Land Company. This company began selling off parcels of its land three years later, and by 1807 a man named Alfred Pierpont Edwards had purchased South Bass, Middle Bass, and Gibraltar for approximately $25,000.

In 1811, Edwards's men drove off the French-Canadian squatters who were the first white inhabitants of the area. The following year, about thirty of Edwards's employees cleared three hundred acres of forest on South Bass, erected a building near Put-in-Bay harbor, and began to raise sheep, hogs, potatoes, corn, and wheat.

Meanwhile, the British renewed their claim to the Bass Islands at the onset of the War of 1812, and together with the Indians (who had, by treaty, retained hunting privileges on the islands), they routed the members of the Edwards settlement, burned buildings, and destroyed crops.

The British claim to the Bass Islands was but part of a larger interest in all of the Northwest Territory, and as a result, a number of important battles were fought in northwestern Ohio. One of the most significant of these was the Battle of Lake Erie. This three-hour naval confrontation, on 10 September 1813, resulted in the defeat and capture of a British naval squadron by the American commodore, Oliver Hazard Perry. During the conflict, giant clouds of cannon smoke were easily seen from the Bass Islands, and Perry used South Bass's Put-in-Bay as a base of operations, while nearby Gibraltar Island reportedly served as a lookout. Six British and American naval officers were killed during the battle and buried at what now is known as the Island Park. According to local legend, a single willow tree sprouted from a tiny sprig dropped on the gravesite. After the willow died, the Cannonball Monument was erected.

Two years later, as a result of the Treaty of Ghent, the British permanently gave up all claims to the Bass Islands. In the meantime, Edwards's heirs continued to employ agents to settle and farm the area, especially South Bass, where the first permanent settlement was established in 1822 near Put-in-Bay harbor. Timbering began on all the islands, which were rich in oak, walnut, and cedar, and by 1837, Edwards's representatives had begun cutting and selling cedar wood as steamship fuel. The islands' native limestone also was sold as ship ballast.

Yet although habitation and commerce had begun, development of the islands was slow to occur. Ships came and went, a few docks were built, and passengers occasionally stopped to view the pleasing island scenery. By 1853, only five or six families lived permanently on the islands in a handful of cabins.

In 1854, settlement began in earnest when a Puerto Rican

named José de Rivera Saint Jurgo bought South Bass, Middle Bass, and Gibraltar from Edwards's heir, Alice Edwards Vinton. De Rivera, as he is commonly known, had toured America's southern states with the intention of buying land for a plantation, but was put off by the idea of slavery. Hearing of the beauty of the Lake Erie islands, he chartered a boat to Put-in-Bay and within forty-eight hours owned the three islands that the Edwards family had held for nearly half a century.

De Rivera first raised sheep on South Bass, but he soon became interested in cultivating grapes. Expounding on the islands' favorable climate and soil conditions, he managed to interest several German wine-growing experts from Cincinnati and the old country in his scheme. The first vines were planted in 1858, and by 1865, grape varieties such as Concord, Niagara, and Amber Queen were cultivated in the islands, and sixty thousand pounds of grapes were being harvested annually. As the island wine industry prospered, land prices soared to $1,500 per acre. In 1871, the Put-in-Bay Wine Company was formed to represent no fewer than forty local vintners, shippers, and distributors. And by 1878, South Bass alone boasted seventy-one grape growers cultivating 550 acres.

Among the pioneers who purchased land for grape growing from de Rivera are important names in Bass Island history such as Ruh, Mueller, Burggraf, Wehrle, Dodge, Vroman, and Cooper. But perhaps the name most known outside the islands was that of John Brown, Jr., son of the famous abolitionist and Harpers Ferry raider. He settled and began raising grapes on South Bass after his father was executed in 1859; he is buried in the island's Crown Hill Cemetery. Today several of the old-fashioned wine cellars built by the pioneer families still stand, but many of the family vineyards have been bought by large companies such as Meier's. A few family vineyards do, however, remain in operation.

As the mellow local wines gained in reputation, so did interest in the islands' pleasant scenery. Soon passenger steamers from Toledo, Sandusky, Detroit, and Cleveland began to dock at various wineries and shaded inlets, and especially at Put-in-Bay harbor. The island area became known as a restful summer retreat, and wealthy and prominent figures including Presidents Hayes, Cleveland, Harrison, and Taft visited the Bass Islands. Stores, restaurants, hotels, and taverns were built for the eager tourists, who crowded the steamers daily in warm weather, and the rich built lavish summer homes, joined elegant private clubs, or frequented exclusive resorts.

The palatial Hotel Victory on South Bass, which opened in 1892, represented the height of the islands' popularity with tourists. In its day the world's largest summer hotel, the massive structure burned to the ground in 1919; the grandeur of its Victorian-style architecture and its prominence as a summer haven, however, are still well remembered.

Although the days of their turn-of-the-century glory are past, the Bass Islands, and South Bass and Put-in-Bay in particular, have retained their popularity. Today, attractions such as Perry's Monument, the Viking Longhouse, the Lonz Winery, and the Crystal Cave continue to draw visitors, who delight in the relaxed yet festive atmosphere found in the area.

Renewed interest in fishing and boating also have helped fill the hotels, restaurants, and taverns of South and Middle Bass, while the local scenery, quaint architecture, and historic sites add to the region's appeal. As soaring travel costs keep vacationers close to home, tourists are rediscovering the Bass Islands and their fascinating heritage.

TOUR 1
Vintage Village

(1.6 miles)

1. The Island Park
   (also known as
   De Rivera Park)
2. The Carriage House
3. The Schlitz Ice House
4. The Crescent Tavern
5. The Round House
6. The Park Hotel
7. The Country House
8. Frosty's
9. The Colonial
10. The Kite Shop
11. Heritage Antiques/
    The Lone Willow
12. The Town Hall
13. The Blacksmith Shop
14. Tony's Place
15. The Put-in-Bay School

16. The Gascoyne
    House
17. Saint Paul's
    Episcopal Church
18. Mother of Sorrows
    Catholic Church
19. The Idlor House
20. Ted's Tackle Shop
21. The Wharf Side
    (The Yacht Shop)
22. The Doller Colonial
    House
23. The Doller Villa
24. The Crew's Nest
25. The Dodge House
26. The Put-in-Bay
    Yacht Club
27. The Warren Cottage

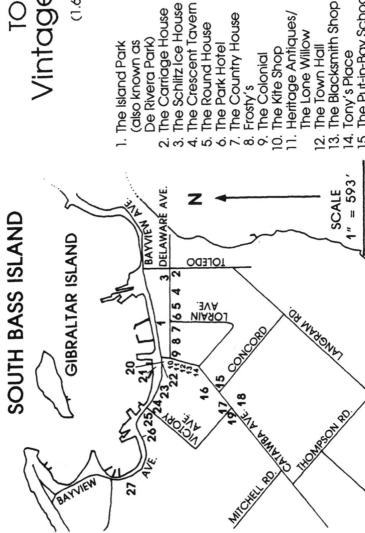

SOUTH BASS ISLAND

GIBRALTAR ISLAND

BAYVIEW AVE.

DELAWARE AVE.

TOLEDO

LORAIN AVE.

CONCORD

LANGRAM RD.

VICTORY AVE.

CATAWBA AVE.

MITCHELL RD.

THOMPSON RD.

BAYVIEW AVE.

N

SCALE
1" = 593'

TOUR ONE
Vintage Village

(1.6 MILES)

Considerable dispute exists about the origin of the name "Put-in-Bay." Some say it derives from "pudding bay," an epithet applied to the harbor by early visitors because it was soft-bottomed and shaped like a pudding bag. Others claim the name was given to the inlet by early navigators who considered it the best place to "put in" between Buffalo and the Detroit River. Whatever the source of its name, the harbor village, which celebrated its centennial in 1977, today offers an interesting array of historical architecture, as well as a glimpse at the growth of a resort community that has hosted promenading ladies and gentlemen, suntanned boaters, and local entrepreneurs who developed the tourist trade.

Delaware Avenue

1. The Island Park (officially known as De Rivera Park). We begin this three-part tour by strolling through the Delaware Avenue commercial district, which is the heart of Put-in-Bay village. At the center of this district is Island Park, which is also known as De Rivera Park after the man who was the father of the Bass Island wine industry. This cool, shady grove has provided a resting place for summer visitors since de Rivera deeded it to the public in 1866. At the west end of Island Park stands the pyramid-shaped Cannonball Monument, which marks the former gravesite of six naval officers who died in 1813 during the Battle of Lake Erie. The park offers a charming view of the harbor; it also features a refreshing rubble-and-fieldstone fountain and a double-faced cast-iron street clock made by Boston's famous E. Howard Company. Adjoining the park is Harbour Square, which opened for business in June of 1986 as a collection of shops. Each shop has its own architectural design which reflects the type of business. For

The Island Park

example, Stonehenge, which sells gifts from England, has a brick front, and Sundae's, an ice cream store, has stained glass windows in its store front. There are many other businesses within the square, including the Chamber of Commerce.

2. The Carriage House. On the south side of Delaware Avenue, east of Island Park, stands a simple frame structure with a Gothic peaked roof; it was built about 1905 by John Brick and first housed a saloon. Later the building became part of the E and K (Engel and Krudwig) Winery, of Sandusky, Ohio, and after that, the home of the Put-in-Bay Golf Club. Today this large commercial edifice houses a gift shop.

The Carriage House

3. The Schlitz Ice House. Across Delaware Avenue from the Carriage House is the turn-of-the-century ice house that once supplied the island's hotels. The building was purchased by the Schlitz Brewing Company in 1913, when they acquired the nearby Beebe House hotel, which later was destroyed by fire. The thick sawdust-insulated walls of the structure made it especially efficient. It was used to store the ice, cut in blocks from the frozen bay in winter, until it was needed during the summer. On the roof, the headhouse is still visible; it once contained the pulley that hauled huge blocks of ice through the access doors that run up the front of the building. It now houses a gift shop.

4. The Crescent Tavern. Crossing Delaware Avenue once again, we see the hotel built in 1871 by Great Lakes sea captain Rear Admiral J. J. Hunker and his wife, Mary. Hunker was a graduate of the U.S. Naval Academy who distinguished himself in the

Ice Cutting

Spanish-American War by capturing Cuba's Nipe Bay in 1898. After the Hunkers' ownership, the structure was known as Ward's Summer Resort and later, the Detroit House. In the early 1920s, it became the Crescent Hotel and was operated by retired actor T. B. Alexander and his wife, Edith Brown Alexander, the granddaughter of John Brown of Harpers Ferry fame. After exterior and interior renovation, it was reopened as the Crescent Tavern in 1981. The ornate roofline brackets and narrow windows make this building an excellent example of the Italianate style of architecture, which flourished in the Bass Islands between 1860 and 1890.

The Crescent Tavern

The Round House Bar and Park Hotel

5. The Round House. Continuing west along Delaware Avenue we come to the Round House. Some say it was originally built in Toledo and reassembled in Put-in-Bay in 1873; others maintain it was built on the island. Perfectly round with a circumference of 150 feet, the structure first housed the Columbia Restaurant in 1873. For many years after it opened, island residents would gather on the front steps yearly at summer's end to pose for a group portrait; this traditional photograph came to be known as the "Mossback Picture" because the islanders were called "mossbackers" for living on a "rock." The tradition was revived in 1982. The Round House remains one of the island's most popular night spots.

6. The Park Hotel. Next door to the Round House is the Park Hotel, originally the Deutsches Hotel, built at about the same time and by the same person, "Round House" Smith. One of the oldest continuously operating hotels in Ohio, it is the last hotel still operating in the village's commercial area. The hotel consists of an eastern portion that was constructed in 1873 and connects with the Round House, and a western addition that more than doubled the hotel's size when it was built in 1887. The tall corner tower at the building's west end and its wrap-around porch are typical of the Italian Villa architectural style seen in many island structures, but the sloping mansard roof and narrow dormer windows give it a Second French Empire flavor, as well. Also of interest is the original lobby, which features outstanding nineteenth-century etched- and stained-glass windows. In the courtyard sits a gleaming antique popcorn wagon made in Oldtown, Maine, in 1909.

7. The Country House. Moving along the avenue we arrive at a building called the Country House, formerly the Gill House, the Bon-Air, the Central Hotel, the Smith Hotel, and the Hotel Oelschlager. It was operated as a hotel by various proprietors for about two decades after 1885 and is now a gift shop. Like the Crescent Tavern, it is Italianate in style, with narrow windows and roof brackets. Its ornate, rounded cornice and molded windows once overlooked a broad front porch. Inside the building is a finely carved staircase and extensive ornamental woodwork known as fretwork.

View of Main Street in 1906

The Colonial, destroyed by fire in May 1988

8. Frosty's. Adjacent to the Country House is the only brick commercial structure in Put-in-Bay's business district. It was built in 1913 by Karl Oelschlager, to house the Oelschlager's Dry Goods Store. It has served as a dry goods store, a gift shop, and an ice cream parlor; it is now a pizza shop that is popular with island tourists. The interior offers a nostalgic atmosphere with its original hardwood floors and floral-design pressed-tin ceiling.

9. The Colonial. The original building at the corner of Delaware and Catawba avenues was for some 80 years perhaps the most recognizable of Put-in-Bay's architectural offerings. Monumental in scale, the Colonial was built by island promoters in 1905 and originally housed a bowling alley, a restaurant, a bar, and a second-floor dance hall boasting 18,000 square feet of open space. Its architectural features included the unusual domed and rounded corner pavilion and the broad porch. The building was destroyed by fire on May 27, 1988, and reopened twelve months later. The rebuilt Colonial, like the original, houses the Beer Barrel Saloon, along with a restaurant and shops. Its architecture, however, is post-modern with Art Deco influences.

Catawba Avenue

10. The Kite Shop. The next leg of the Vintage Village tour takes us through the commercial district and residential area of Catawba

Avenue. First we see an 1870 structure that originally housed a shoe-repair shop and a store run by Chris Doller, the brother of South Bass Island's wealthy mayor, Valentine Doller. The structure that once housed Chris Doller's shop is now a residence and gift shop. Its architecture shows an interesting blend of simple Greek Revival lines and decorative Italianate molding.

11. Heritage Antiques / The Lone Willow. The next stop on Catawba Avenue is at an antique and gift shop that was built about 1880 as the Schiele Building; for many years, its upper floor served as the meeting hall of the Independent Order of Odd Fellows, or I.O.O.F. The local I.O.O.F. order called themselves the Lone Willow Chapter because the building faced the Island Park burial site of the six British and American naval officers killed in the Battle of Lake Erie. The building is a simple frame structure with an unusual second-story central window in the Queen Anne style. Above this, the ornate cornice with its diagonal and vertical board patterns is characteristic of the Stick Style of architectural design popular in the 1880s and 1890s.

12. The Town Hall. Constructed in 1887 at a cost of $10,127 by local builder George Gascoyne, this is one of the few brick buildings on the Bass Islands. It was erected on land donated to

The Wolkersdorfer Building

The Town Hall

the village by the wealthy Valentine Doller; the structure originally housed a jail in its basement, police and fire departments
on its first floor, and a stage and basketball facility in its upper
story. Today it is still the home of the local police department,
and community events are held on the second floor; the fire
department is now housed in the building next door. The Town
Hall was once marked by a large wooden open belfry, which no
longer graces the southern tower. The building's original
decorative slate roof remains and is worth noting.

13. The Blacksmith Shop. This was South Bass Island's first
service station. Built in 1911 by William Kunzler, this village shop
also offered automobile repair. For many years, the building was
allowed to fall into disrepair until it was purchased in 1968,
restored, and opened as a gift shop and museum of South Bass
artifacts and memorabilia. The structure is unusual because its
entire front is covered with stamped tin resembling decorative
brick.

A Put-in-Bay tour bus in front of the school, 1920s

14. Tony's Place. Located next door to the Blacksmith Shop, this building has housed a bar or restaurant ever since its construction at the turn of the century. Architecturally it is a simple frame structure, but the Dutch "shaped gable" on the building's upper face is an interesting feature.

15. The Put-in-Bay School. Crossing the street at the corner of Concord Avenue, we see the schoolhouse designed by G. E. Scott and constructed by J. A. Feick, of Sandusky. Built in 1921 after a special bond issue was passed by local citizens in 1919, the schoolhouse originally contained ten rooms and was considered quite modern for its time. The school still serves the islanders' educational needs. It is simple in design, with stone relieving the monotony of its brick wall surfaces.

16. The Gascoyne House. Across the street from the school is the home of prominent island citizen and local builder George Gascoyne. He was the designer of the village's Town Hall, the island's leading contractor, and served the community as councilman, fire chief, and postmaster at various times. His house is surprisingly modest in style and proportion and offers little hint that its builder designed some of the island's most stylish buildings. This building currently houses a tourist home called Lake Erie Islands House.

17. Saint Paul's Episcopal Church. At the corner of Catawba and Lake View avenues stands Saint Paul's Church, built in 1865 on land donated by José de Rivera. Jay Cooke, another wealthy philanthropist who at one time owned Gibraltar Island, underwrote the building's cost. The church continues to serve the area. The frame structure is symmetrical in plan and Gothic in design, with a steep roof line and pointed windows; its vertically ribbed exterior walls are typical of the board-and-batten style of Gothic architecture.

18. Mother of Sorrows Catholic Church. Across Catawba is Saint Paul's Catholic counterpart, which in 1927 replaced a simpler, smaller-frame Catholic church that had been built about 1875. The present structure was designed by the Reverend Joseph Maerder, a church pastor who used an airplane to travel around the islands to conduct Sunday services. The Reverend Maerder's design was based on a similar building in Lombardy, Italy, and his plans were executed by architect Howard Gorman. The church is Romanesque in style, constructed of Kelleys Island limestone, and

The original Catholic Church

The Catholic Church

features a lovely Florentine marble altar. Above its main entrance is a delicate rose window.

19. Idlor House. After crossing Catawba again, we see another of George Gascoyne's designs. The structure dates from 1875 and is considered one of his finest residential buildings. Erected for storekeeper and dockmaster Clinton Idlor, the building's bracketed roofline, carved porch woodwork, and bay window make it a fine example of Italianate architecture. Inside, decorative woodwork and the original wallpaper are of interest.

Bayview Avenue

20. Ted's Tackle Shop. Retracing our steps along Catawba Avenue, we begin the third and final part of our Vintage Village tour. As we stroll westward on Bayview Avenue, we enjoy breathtaking views of the harbor while discovering more about island history and the enterprising Valentine Doller. At the corner of Catawba and Bayview is a structure built by him in 1873. He originally opened the building as a saloon, store, and post office (he was island postmaster from 1860 to 1876), and his name graces the building's façade. Soon afterward Clinton Idlor kept shop here, from 1876 to 1892. The structure is another example of the Italianate architectural style so popular in the islands, and

The Idlor House

The Corner Store

although its walls have recently been covered with aluminum siding, it displays the bracketed roof parapet typical of the Italianate design. The Doller Building previously housed the Corner Store and now houses Reflections. The Corner Store is currently located south of Tony's Place and the Put-in-Bay School (see Tour 1, Stops 14 and 15).

21. The Wharf Side (also known as the Yacht Shop). Across the street on the waterfront stands another Doller structure. The frame portion of this building was a part of Doller's boathouse and dock. In its heyday, about 1872, Doller's dock was often crowded by

An interior view of the Corner Store

Ships at the Doller Dock, 1872

steamboats. Raised and remodeled in 1986, the Yacht Shop effectively ties the old and new buildings together without damaging the area's historical appeal.

22. The Doller Colonial House. Behind the commercial building on the corner of Bayview and Catawba stands a white Colonial Revival style residence. Doller and his wife had six daughters, five of whom never married, and this house was built by some of the Doller daughters in 1932. The unusual rounded canopy over the main door is an interesting feature.

23. The Doller Villa. Next door to the Doller Colonial House is the spectacular private residence built by Valentine Doller about 1870. Valentine, a clever and successful tourist-industry entrepreneur, bought José de Rivera's remaining island holdings when de Rivera went bankrupt in the 1880s. The mansion bears some resemblance to Inselruhe, another grand home, which we shall see in Tour 3. Doller lived here until his death in 1901. Like Inselruhe, and the Park Hotel seen earlier, the house is an example of Italian Villa architecture, typified by its large, octagonal corner tower. Other interesting details include the tower's iron cresting or railing, and the home's broad wrap-around porch. The brick portion of the Doller Villa was added later to the original frame structure.

24. The Crew's Nest. Located at the corner of Bayview and Victory avenues, this building and the private residence just to its east were both built about 1875 and recall the picket-fence days of nineteenth-century Put-in-Bay. The Crew's Nest, formerly the Eagle Cottage Hotel and the Friendly Inn, was remodeled and became a private club in 1971; the bedside night tables from the old hotel are now used in the club's downstairs bar. The club and the residence, with their roof brackets and broad porches, are typical of the island's Italianate cottage design.

25. The Dodge House. On the opposite corner of Victory Avenue stands the home built about 1870 by Captain Elliot Dodge; the finely preserved residence remains in the Dodge family. Considered by many as one of the best examples of Italianate architecture on the islands, it has a broad wrap-around veranda and decorative moldings around its windows and doors.

26. The Put-in-Bay Yacht Club. Situated at the spot where Bayview Avenue begins to curve to the southwest, this edifice was constructed in 1924. The Yacht Club, however, traces its existence to 1886. Covered with stucco and sporting large,

The Doller Villa

The Crew's Nest

curving arches, the building shows the influence of Spanish-style architecture. The club annually hosts the Inter-Lake Yachting Association Regatta.

27. The Warren Cottage. This is one of four cottages beyond the Yacht Club that typify the work of skilled "cottage carpenters" of the late 1800s. The Warren residence, also known as La Rosa, was built about 1893. The board-and-batten and circular woodwork on its front gable are unique; the steep roof and vertical design of the front gable recall Saint Paul's Church.

The Dodge House

The Warren Cottage

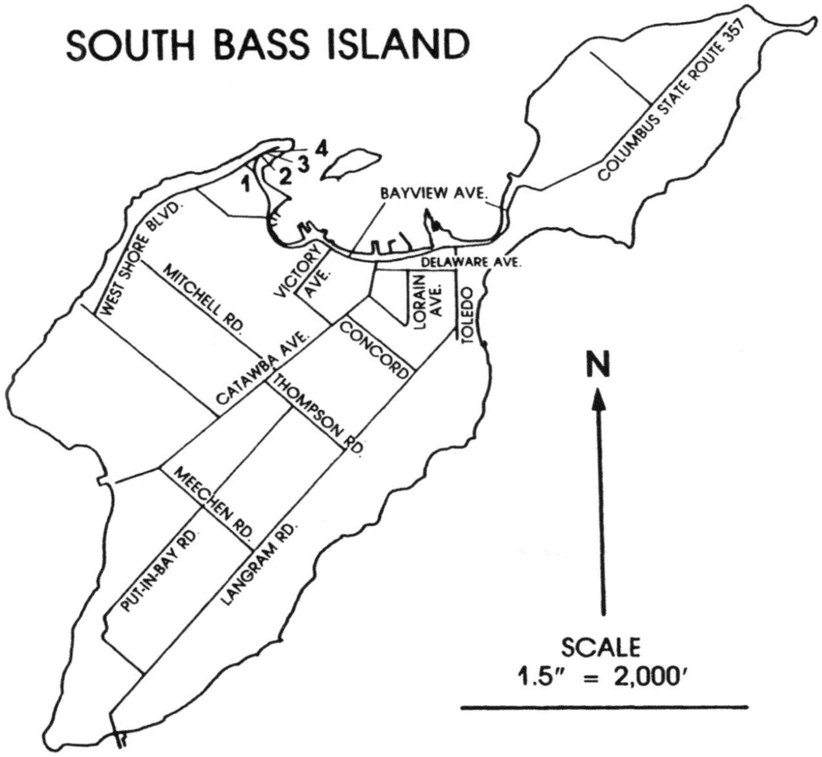

SOUTH BASS ISLAND

TOUR 2
Science & Serenity
(0.2 miles)

1. The Bayview House
2. The Stone Laboratory Research Station
3. The State Fish Hatchery
4. The Feick Cottage

N

SCALE
1.5" = 2,000'

COLUMBUS STATE ROUTE 357

BAYVIEW AVE.
DELAWARE AVE.
TOLEDO
LORAIN AVE.
CONCORD
VICTORY AVE.
THOMPSON RD.
CATAWBA AVE.
MITCHELL RD.
WEST SHORE BLVD.
MEECHEN RD.
LANGRAM RD.
PUT-IN-BAY RD.

TOUR TWO
Science and Serenity

(0.2 MILES)

As Bayview Avenue winds northward, the bustle of Put-in-Bay village fades to the quiet serenity of Peach Point. Originally a peach orchard developed by José de Rivera, the area later became the site of the Federal Fish Hatchery, which was constructed in 1889. A decade or so later, a number of small, frame cottages were built at Peach Point for artists and writers visiting the islands. During the next fifteen years, the State of Ohio began establishing its own fish hatcheries here, and The Ohio State University located a biological research station in the State Hatchery Building in 1918. Ohio State's local research facilities are currently known as Franz Theodore Stone Laboratory—or simply as Stone Lab. The headquarters of Stone Lab are on Gibraltar Island, and it now owns the former Federal Hatchery. In addition to its tranquillity and its scientific attractions, Peach Point also offers some of the island's best views of the harbor and Perry's Monument, especially at night.

1. The Bayview House. The second cottage on Bayview Avenue at Peach Point, this simple, square, frame structure was built about 1900. In 1940, the house became the property of Thomas and Marina Langlois; Thomas Langlois was the distinguished director of Stone Lab for many years. The building currently houses Stone Lab's main office and library. The simple, shingle construction of the home is indicative of its catalog design.

2. The Stone Laboratory Research Station. Going north along Bayview we come to what was the Federal Fish Hatchery building designed by the popular island contractor George Gascoyne and built in 1889. The horizontal and vertical boards applied to the projecting gables make this a fine example of Stick Style archi-

Oak Point, 1914

tecture, popular during the last two decades of the 1800s. Surrounding the hatchery are several small cottages that house Stone Lab's summer faculty, students, and guests.

3. The State Fish Hatchery. Just next door to the Stone Lab facility, the State Fish Hatchery continues to serve as a fish breeding station. This building was constructed in 1925 to

The Research Station

Fish & Game Hatchery, 1907

replace another state hatchery that was destroyed by fire the preceding year. The first State Fish Hatchery building was built in 1907 on the former site of the Forest City Ice Company. The present two-story brick structure with cement and stucco trim is architecturally similar to the Put-in-Bay School on Catawba Avenue. Both buildings were erected by the J. A. Feick Con-

State Fish Hatchery, now

The Feick Cottage

struction Company, of Sandusky, Ohio. Tours of the State Fish
Hatchery are offered by appointment.

4. The Feick Cottage. Immediately next to the State
Hatchery stands the cottage residence built by the Feick family
in 1901. The Feick Construction Company erected numerous
island landmarks; in addition to the State Hatchery just seen,
they include the Put-in-Bay School and the famous Hotel
Victory, which we shall see in Tour 5. The company traces its
operations back to the 1850s. It is reportedly one of the oldest
continuously operating construction companies in the nation. A
Colonial Revival-style cottage, the dwelling features an elliptical
second-story window and walls covered with wood shingles.

TOUR 3
In the Shadow of
Perry's Monument

(1 mile)

1. Perry's Victory and International
   Peace Memorial
2. The Hunker Villa
3. Inselruhe
4. The Acorn Club
5. The Ruh House
6. The Henry Burggraf Farm
7. The Matthias Burggraf Farm

SOUTH BASS ISLAND

COLUMBUS STATE
ROUTE 357

BAYVIEW AVE.

DELAWARE AVE.

LORAIN AVE.

TOLEDO

CONCORD

VICTORY AVE.

THOMPSON RD.

CATAWBA AVE.

MITCHELL RD.

LANGRAM RD.

MEECHEN RD.

PUT-IN-BAY RD.

WEST SHORE BLVD.

N

SCALE
1.5" = 2,000'

TOUR THREE
In the Shadow of Perry's Monument

(1 MILE)

Separated from the village by the narrow strip of land that supports Perry's Victory and International Peace Memorial, East Point is home for several old island families. Predominantly agricultural, the area has been dotted with vineyards since it was settled by the German families of Ruh, Burggraf, and Mueller in the mid-1880s; many of these early vintners' farmhouses can still be seen along State Route 357. The entry to East Point along Bayview Avenue passes by Perry's large granite monument and is marked by two of the most elaborate "cottages" found on the Lake Erie islands.

1. Perry's Victory and International Peace Memorial. This towering granite column rises 352 feet above Lake Erie and commemorates the decisive naval victory of Commodore Oliver Hazard Perry over the British at the Battle of Lake Erie during the War of 1812. The memorial was dedicated at the centennial celebration of the battle on 10 September 1913 and was originally known as the Perry Victory Monument. The current name was adopted in 1972 to recognize the fact that the structure also symbolizes the continuing peace between the United States and Canada. The bodies of the six American and British naval officers who died during the battle were moved from their original graves in Island Park to the base of this monument during its construction in 1913. The memorial column is Roman Doric in design and is one of the tallest such towers in the world. An open promenade at the top can be reached by elevator and offers a spectacular view of Put-in-Bay harbor, the Ohio mainland, Michigan, Canada, and various Erie islands. The column is crowned by a bronze tripod measuring approximately twenty feet by seventeen feet. It was designed by the architect J. H. Freedlander and cast by the

Perry's Victory and
International Peace Memorial

The Bronze Tripod

Gorham Bronze Company. The monument was renovated by the
U.S. Department of the Interior in the early 1980s and regularly
offers tours and period military exhibitions in the summer months.

Construction begins

Setting stone,
close-up

Setting stone

Ground breaking ceremony with Governor Harmon

2. The Hunker Villa. Located across a wide expanse of lawn next to the monument, this imposing summer home reportedly was built in 1870 for Mrs. Mary Lockwood and was known as the Lockwood Villa. Much later, prominent islander Mary Monroe Hunker lived here after the death of her husband, Rear Admiral J. J. Hunker, in 1916. The Italian Villa style of the dwelling is characterized by the long windows and by the square tower that juts a full story above the building's roofline. At the top of the tower, an open railing encloses what is called a "Captain's Walk."

3. Inselruhe. Directly north of the Hunker Villa is another impressive home; this one bears the name Inselruhe, which in German means "Island Rest." This building was designed by Toledo architect James Young for James B. Monroe, a Toledo railroad magnate; it was constructed by the popular island builder George Gascoyne in 1875. Monroe's daughter was Mary Monroe Hunker, who occupied Inselruhe with her husband be-

The Hunker Villa

Inselruhe

fore moving to the Hunker Villa next door after her husband's death. This structure's impressive design, sometimes known as "Steamboat Gothic," is a variation of Italian Villa architecture. Again we see a corner tower (octagonal in this case), long narrow windows, and a broad veranda. The building also features decorative woodwork, moldings, and brackets, along with iron and wooden cresting (roof railings). A variety of interesting and ornate outbuildings is also found on the property. The estate's present owners have arranged with the National Trust for Historic Preservation to protect and maintain this outstanding vintage summer home.

4. The Acorn Club. Bayview Avenue now takes a sharp right and becomes Chapman Road. Off Chapman a left turn leads to Columbus Avenue (State Route 357), where the Acorn Club soon comes into view. Built by Joseph Tyler about 1870, the structure is now a sportsmen's club. The building is interesting for the way

The Acorn Club

it combines the simplicity of the Greek Revival style with the more elaborate elements of Italianate architecture such as the large central cupola and the bracketed roofline.

5. The Ruh House. Across Columbus Avenue is the 1870 home built by German vintner and island pioneer Karl Ruh. The house is flanked by a smokehouse, a press house, and a board-and-batten barn; only two families have owned the property since the dwelling was first built. Very similar to the Acorn Club in its blend of Greek Revival and Italianate features, the Ruh House is a symmetrical, boxlike structure with Italianate brackets but without a cupola.

6. The Henry Burggraf Farm. Farther out along State Route 357 are two farmsteads of the Burggraf family. These early settlers first came from Baden, Germany, to Kelleys Island, but moved to South Bass in 1859, where they established vineyards and a winery. Members of the family became prominent citizens, and Mathias Burggraf served as school superintendent and township trustee. The Henry Burggraf farmhouse was originally built by his parents, Anna and Mathias, Sr., about 1865 or 1870. The farm is still owned by Burggraf descendants. The dwelling is of Italianate design with long, narrow windows and intricate geometric wood

Board-and-batten Barn

patterns on the small front porch; the stucco-covered walls are scored to resemble stone block. The wooded lot also contains several interesting outbuildings, such as the long, sloping-roofed barn with its board-and-batten siding.

7. The Matthias Burggraf Farm. A short distance from the Henry Burggraf Farm is the farm where Anna and Mathias Burggraf resided until 1921. Built in 1898, the large Queen Anne farmhouse is typically asymmetrical in plan and features a high roof and a broad front porch. Other noteworthy details of the Queen Anne style seen here are the large picture-type window and the double-paned window of the front gable.

TOUR 4
Vineyards and Vikings

(3.9 miles)

1. The Engel Farm
2. The Stone Wine Press
3. The Alois Niele House (also known as the Wiesler House)
4. The George Bickford House
5. The Reibel House Hotel
6. The Foster Farm
7. The Daniel Vroman House
8. The Philip Vroman House
9. Cooper's Restaurant
10. The Mortimer Wine Press
11. The José de Rivera Estate
12. The Mammoth Cave
13. The Heineman Winery and Crystal Cave
14. The Charles Miller House
15. The de Rivera Wine Facilities
16. The Viking Longhouse

SOUTH BASS ISLAND

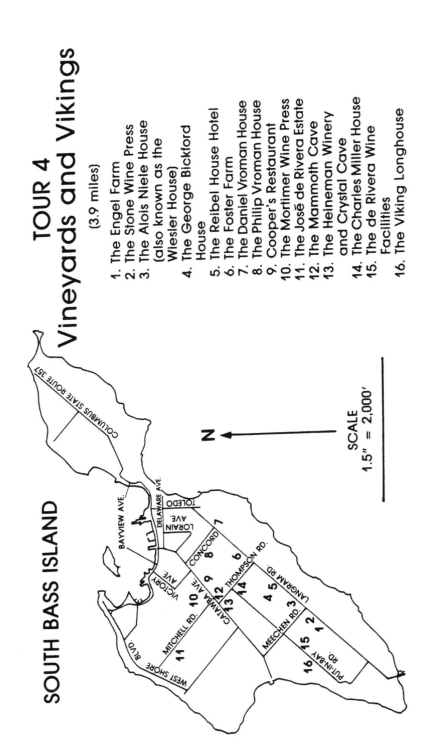

N

SCALE
1.5" = 2,000'

TOUR FOUR
Vineyards and Vikings

(3.9 MILES)

A series of limestone caverns crisscrosses the center of South Bass Island near the intersection of Catawba Avenue and Thompson Road. Crystal Cave at Heineman's Winery, Perry's Cave, and Mammoth Cave (no longer open to the public) are among the best known of these; such underground attractions have added to the romance and intrigue of the island over the years, and they also offer a cool retreat on sultry summer days. Prior to leading past the caves, Tour 4 starts along the southern stretch of Airport (or Langram) Road—the main thoroughfare from the Lime Kiln Dock to the village—across from the airport. The tour takes us to some of the South Bass Island vineyards that were established in the 1860s by German grape-growing pioneers who purchased land from José de Rivera; many early farmhouses and stone press houses can be viewed from the roadway. Tour 4 ends at the secluded Viking Longhouse.

1. The Engel Farm. One of the few island properties to stay in the same family is the Engel Farm, first settled by Christian Engel. He immigrated to the United States from Saxony, Germany, in 1840, and in 1868 arrived at South Bass, where he soon established a sprawling vineyard. The production of grapes has been carried on by his son Christian, grandson Herbert, and great-grandson Robert, who currently owns the farm. The farmhouse was built in 1872, and a boulder in the front yard bears a plaque commemorating the 1972 centennial. The home is an L-shaped Italianate structure with clean lines and peaked moldings over the doors and windows. Behind the main dwelling is a frame winepress house. Press buildings, where grapes were processed for their juice, can still be seen on many island farms. Usually the pressing took place on the ground floor, and the fermentation that

The Stone Wine Press

changed the juice into wine occurred below in a stone cellar. The current tour will pass several wine-press houses, but a particularly fine example is the Press House Bait Store which we shall see in Tour 5.

2. The Stone Wine Press. Following Langram Road toward the village, just before Meechen Road we see a cluster of trees set back from the highway. The trees shade a renovated stone press house that is now a private residence; the once prosperous vineyards that kept workers busy in this press house are now runways for the nearby airport. Built by English stonemason Alfred Parker, who came to South Bass in 1865, the press's walls are massive and rough and the cellar bears a gabled entrance.

3. The Alois Niele House (also known as the Wiesler House). Past Meechen Road is another of the island's rare brick structures. This one was built around 1870 of brick shipped from the mainland. The building sat vacant and decaying for many years but was renovated in 1979 and now houses a shop. Long narrow windows and bracketed cornices indicate the Italianate style, as do the ornate window moldings and the restored bay window on the house's north side.

4. The George Bickford House. This residence was built about 1868 by a vintner and township trustee. Set well back from the road amid the overgrown vineyards that once supported its owner, the building is L-shaped and Italianate in design.

The Niele House

5. The Reibel House Hotel. In contrast to the Bickford House, the Reibel House stands in a clearing near the road. The property was bought in the 1880s by German native Henry Reibel and was owned by his heirs until 1954. The Reibel House was once a rambling forty-room inn that stood surrounded by vineyards and orchards. The building's construction date is disputed, but the structure may have already existed in 1882 when Reibel bought the land. An 1864 penny found in a door frame during renovation suggests that the structure was built during the Civil War era. Gothic peaks on the front gable and a wide Italian Villa type wrap-around porch are examples of the mid-1800s tendency to mix architectural styles.

The Reibel Hotel

The Foster House

6. The Foster Farm. Just past Thompson Road, the two stone structures of the Foster Farm—the farmhouse and the press house—mark it as a typical example of mid-nineteenth century island farms. Both buildings date from about 1860 and are made of rubble stone; they are attributed to English stonemason Alfred Parker, who built the Stone Press House seen earlier. The press house has wood trim, peaked window moldings, and a small, gabled cellar entrance. The house is a stone version of the island's familiar L-shaped farmhouses.

7. The Daniel Vroman House. Located opposite the end of Concord Avenue, this residence was built around 1870; it is a good example of the architecture of its period. The dwelling exhibits Gothic elements in its steep roof, and its stylish wooden ornamentation is also worthy of note.

8. The Philip Vroman House. On the south side of Concord, this dwelling was built by Daniel's pioneer father, Philip Vroman, about 1860. Philip arrived on South Bass Island in 1843 and worked for both the Edwards and de Rivera families. One of the earliest island pioneers, he also served as township trustee. The home is now owned by his great-granddaughter. The dwelling is of simple Greek Revival design with a decorative Italianate front porch.

The Phillp Vroman House

9. Cooper's Restaurant. Opened by the wine-producing family of Fred Cooper in 1947, this building was constructed over the former Put-in-Bay Wine Company wine cellar. The restaurant carries into the twentieth century the stone construction typical of earlier island buildings; it is believed to be built of limestone taken from the walls of the demolished Put-in-Bay Winery.

Cooper's Restaurant

Street car at Crystal Cave

10. The Mortimer Wine Press. Across and down the street from Cooper's, near the corner of Mitchell Road, is the wine press built by English vintner E. T. Mortimer, who settled on South Bass in 1869. This simple, frame edifice has a stone cellar and has been converted into a private residence.

11. The José de Rivera Estate. At the far crest of a rolling hill along Mitchell Road is the estate of former island owner José de Rivera; he planted vineyards here in 1858 after much of the Bass Islands' timber had been cut for steamboat fuel. De Rivera commuted between the islands and his New York business offices until 1882, when he made South Bass Island his permanent home. In 1886 the millionaire de Rivera went bankrupt and sold much of his island holdings to Put-in-Bay entrepreneur Valentine Doller. On May 31, 1889, de Rivera died a relatively poor man; he is buried in the island's cemetery. The de Rivera Estate remained in his family until 1912. The estate's ancient house and many interesting outbuildings are Greek Revival and board-and-batten in design; their simple lines are typical of the mid-nineteenth-century construction date. The board-and-batten barn across the street from the residence is probably part of the original farmstead.

12. The Mammoth Cave. We now backtrack along Mitchell Road and return to Catawba Avenue, where, at the corner of

Thompson Road, we find a frame building partly obscured by foliage. This is the former entrance to Daussa's Circular and Labyrinthic Cave, which was originally owned by José de Rivera's daughter. The cave was discovered in 1886 and later renamed Mammoth Cave; it has been closed to the public since 1955. Its entrance led sixty feet underground to an eight-by-sixty-foot lake, a six-hundred-foot circular tunnel, and a huge, open cavern. The concession building that once served as the cave entrance sports an ornate square cupola on its roof.

13. The Heineman Winery and Crystal Cave. Across Thompson Road from the Mammoth Cave building is South Bass Island's only operating winery. Now run by third and fourth generation Heineman family winemakers, the facility offers tours of its modern operations and of Crystal Cave during the summer. Discovered in 1897, the cave has numerous interconnecting chambers and, like a giant geode, features numerous unusual strontium crystal formations of various sizes. Yet another cavern, Perry's Cave, is located directly across from the winery on Catawba Avenue. According to local tradition, this cave was discovered by Commodore Perry's men and used by them for the storage of supplies prior to the Battle of Lake Erie.

14. The Charles Miller House. Farther down Thompson, at the corner of Put-in-Bay Road, is the restored home built by German vintner Charles Miller shortly after 1847. Another of the area's

Perry's Cave

early German settlers, Miller (Mueller in German) came to South Bass in 1865. His former residence is Italianate in style, and its peaked window moldings are decorated with floral ornaments.

15. The de Rivera Wine Facilities. We continue along Put-in-Bay Road to a small clearing in the woods just past Meechen Road on the highway's east side. Here is the de Rivera wine-producing complex. No longer used for wine making, the cluster of out-buildings includes a board-and-batten barn that has occupied the site since at least 1874.

16. The Viking Longhouse. A bit farther along Put-in-Bay Road is the final stop on this tour, and perhaps the most unusual attraction in the islands. Erected by Eadwerd and Joyce Hyl, the Viking Longhouse is an eighty-percent scale model reproduction of a traditional Viking barracks. Neither historic nor native to the island in origin, the structure was built using ancient Viking construction techniques: tons of beautiful white pine were joined by the mortise-and-tenon method as the Longhouse was put together barn-raising style between April and August of 1980. Mounds of earth and an earth-covered gateway mark the authentic entrance to the Longhouse, which also serves as a workshop and museum for sculptor Hyl's artworks. Hyl and his wife conduct tours through the fascinating complex during the summer months.

The wine-producing complex

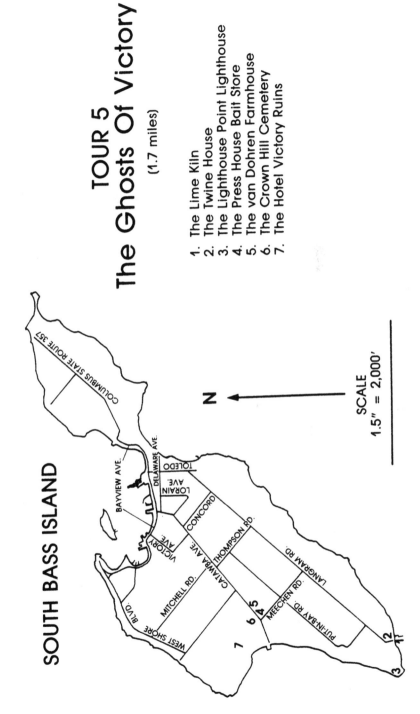

TOUR 5
The Ghosts Of Victory

(1.7 miles)

1. The Lime Kiln
2. The Twine House
3. The Lighthouse Point Lighthouse
4. The Press House Bait Store
5. The van Dohren Farmhouse
6. The Crown Hill Cemetery
7. The Hotel Victory Ruins

SOUTH BASS ISLAND

COLUMBUS STATE ROUTE 357

BAYVIEW AVE.

DELAWARE AVE.

TOLEDO

LORAIN AVE.

CONCORD

VICTORY AVE.

MITCHELL RD.

CATAWBA AVE.

THOMPSON RD.

LANGRAM RD.

MEECHEN RD.

PUT-IN-BAY RD.

WEST SHORE BLVD.

N

SCALE
1.5" = 2,000'

TOUR FIVE
The Ghosts of Victory

(1.7 MILES)

The island's rugged coastline, from the Miller Lime Kiln Dock to Lighthouse Point and beyond, is usually the first glimpse visitors have of South Bass when arriving by ferry. This tour gives a closer look at the landmarks along the south coast, travels inland to view a wine press, farmhouse, and cemetery, and ends at South Bass State Park, site of the ruins of the monumental Hotel Victory, which dominated the western shore in the late 1800s and early 1900s.

1. The Lime Kiln. At the Miller Boat Line's south shore dock is the Lime Kiln, a decaying, angular limestone structure. The kiln was actually a primitive furnace that was used for burning and reducing limestone to the granular substance that is a component of mortar. The kiln functioned for only a short time during the 1860s. Arched stoking holes can still be seen at its base.

2. The Twine House. East of the dock, in the Miller Boat Line parking lot, stands a large, white frame structure that was built around the turn of the century. Twine houses such as this one were relatively common in coastal areas; they were used to hang fish nets for drying or repairing as well as for winter storage.

3. The Lighthouse Point Lighthouse (usually referred to as the South Bass Light or South Bass Lighthouse). On a rise behind the Lime Kiln is a building constructed in 1897 that originally served as both keeper's residence and lighthouse. A massive brick house is connected to the old light. A replacement light in a nearby steel tower was installed in 1962; it is automatic and thus eliminated the need for a keeper. The Ohio State University now uses the brick building as a residence for Stone Lab staff.

The Lighthouse

4. The Press House Bait Store. We now follow Langram Road to Put-in-Bay Road, where we turn left. The road leads us past the Maple Leaf Cemetery, through a winding, wooded vale, and again past the Viking Longhouse and the de Rivera Wine Facilities. We turn left (west) on Meechen Road, which ends at Catawba, where we see the Press House Bait Store on the northeast corner. Erected in 1865 by German immigrant and vintner Max van Dohren, this is one of the finest examples in the islands of a wine-press house; moreover, the interior of the building still contains some of the original pressing equipment. The structure is board-and-batten in design, with a stone foundation and a gabled cellar entrance.

5. The van Dohren Farmhouse. Adjacent to the Press House is van Dohren's rambling home, which remained in the hands of his descendants until 1978. The long windows and peaked window moldings are typical of the Italianate style.

6. The Crown Hill Cemetery. Across Catawba from the van Dohren farmstead is the fence-lined cemetery that serves as the final resting place of island notables such as José de Rivera, Valentine Doller, and John Brown, Jr. The grave of de Rivera, who originally donated the land for the cemetery, is located near the entrance; the grave marker is of limestone covered with lime

Valentine Doller's Mausoleum

whitewash. In the center of the cemetery, surrounded by a grove of trees, stands Valentine Doller's grand mausoleum. Romanesque in design, it was built in 1905 of both smooth-dressed and rough-hewn granite. The mausoleum is noted for its beautiful carved floral patterns.

7. The Hotel Victory Ruins. Near the end of Catawba Avenue in South Bass Island State Park are the remains of the once palatial Hotel Victory. The original resort site covered one hundred acres, twenty-one of which were reserved for the hotel itself and its

The Hotel Victory

Welcome gathering for President Howard Taft at Hotel Victory, 1908

grounds. The hotel was commissioned by Toledo resort developer James K. Tillotson and a group of investors; together they hired E. O. Fallis, prominent Toledo architect, to design the building. The Feick Construction Company of Sandusky built the massive frame structure, laying its cornerstone in September 1889. The hotel opened for business in 1892, but construction was not entirely completed until 1896. The edifice was once said to be the largest

Main lobby and office at the Hotel Victory, 1908

resort hotel in the world. It was six hundred feet long by three hundred feet deep and boasted more than eight hundred rooms. The auditorium could seat seven hundred; the spacious dining room could serve one thousand people, employing hundreds of waiters, maids, and bellhops. The facility offered its own dentist, tailor, stenographer, and manicurist as well. Numerous parlors, wine cellars, and shops were part of the grand hotel's features,

Grounds of the Hotel Victory showing the Rustic Bridge, 1908.
The swimming pool, ruins of which can still be seen at the State Park, was immediately to the left of the bridge

which also included a greenhouse, photographic darkroom, laundry, livery, barber shop, billiard room, ice cream parlor, and newsstand. The entire project, including furnishings, cost an estimated $750,000, but the hotel changed hands numerous times and was never a financial success. Just twenty-three years after it was completed, the Hotel Victory burned on the evening of 14 August 1919 in a spectacular fire that may have been caused by faulty electrical wiring. The ruins of the glorious, multitowered Queen Anne style structure remain in the park and include the pedestal where the hotel's namesake, a statue of Victory, once stood, an empty, crumbling eight-foot-deep cement swimming pool, and clumps of twisted iron.

Main dining hall, Hotel Victory, seating 800 people

TOUR 6
On "Perry's Lookout"
(0.3 miles)

1. The Franz Theodore Stone Laboratory
2. The Cooke Castle
3. Jay Cooke's Boat House

N

SCALE
2.25" = 1,000'

GIBRALTAR ISLAND

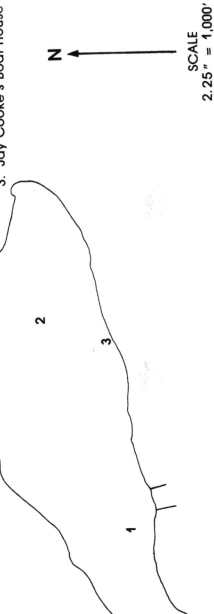

On "Perry's Lookout"
(0.3 MILES)

Tiny Gibraltar Island, which stands in the western part of Put-in-Bay harbor, was named for the rocky Mediterranean headland which it resembles. It has also been called Perry's Lookout, because of the tradition that Commodore Perry stationed men here to watch over his fleet before the Battle of Lake Erie. The island was owned for four decades by Jay Cooke, a Philadelphia banker and Civil War financier, who bought it from José de Rivera for $3,001 in 1864. Cooke regularly visited the island until his death in 1905. In 1925, his heirs sold the island to Columbus industrialist Julius F. Stone, chairman of The Ohio State University's board of trustees. Stone gave the island to the University to use in its biological research around Lake Erie. Stone Lab is one of the oldest and most respected freshwater biology programs in the country, and it currently operates with the Center for Lake Erie Area Research (CLEAR) and the Ohio Sea Grant Program to form the University's Lake Erie program. Gibraltar is easily accessible by boat from Put-in-Bay harbor; prior arrangements to visit must be made with the University.

1. The Franz Theodore Stone Laboratory. The Ohio State University's Lake Erie research facilities were founded in 1896 at Sandusky and later operated at the old Federal Fish Hatchery building at Peach Point. After Julius Stone donated Gibraltar Island to the University for aquatic and biological research in 1925, construction was begun on the laboratory named in honor of Julius's father, Franz Theodore Stone. The building was completed in 1927 and opened for classes the following year; it still houses the main classrooms and laboratories. Standing on the southwestern tip of Gibraltar and overlooking Put-in-Bay harbor, the massive brick structure was designed by Joseph Bradford and

Gibraltar Island

uses reinforced concrete extensively. Other structures, colonial in design, were built on the island in 1929 and 1930 to serve as student residences, dining halls, and recreation areas.

2. The Cooke Castle. At the eastern tip of the island is Jay Cooke's enormous stone residence. Until 1985 the building was used as a men's dorm for Stone Lab students; currently it is being converted to a conference center. This building was constructed shortly after the Civil War, and it was the site of lavish society soirées when Cooke was in residence. Guests included Salmon P. Chase, William T. Sherman, and Rutherford B. Hayes. The castle's design is a variation on Italian Villa architecture; its massive, domed, seven-sided tower is four stories tall, and scrolled brackets line the cornices. Inside, the beautiful decorative features included ornate plasterwork and marble fireplaces. Cooke's spectacular Gothic library in the base of the tower is also well worth seeing. In front of the castle stands the first monument ever erected to honor Commodore Perry's naval victory. The base was laid by the local Battle of Lake Erie Monument Association in 1859; Cooke added the rest of the monument shortly after he bought the island from de Rivera.

3. Jay Cooke's Boat House. Returning to the eastern end of the island, we see the former Cooke Boat House, which has served Ohio State as the Invertebrate Zoology, Ichthyology, and Ecology Lab. The simple board-and-batten structure was built about 1865, soon after Cooke purchased the island.

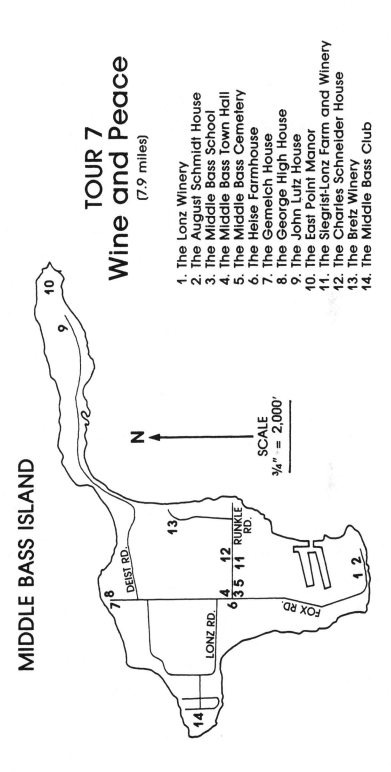

MIDDLE BASS ISLAND

TOUR 7
Wine and Peace
(7.9 miles)

1. The Lonz Winery
2. The August Schmidt House
3. The Middle Bass School
4. The Middle Bass Town Hall
5. The Middle Bass Cemetery
6. The Heise Farmhouse
7. The Gemelch House
8. The George High House
9. The John Lutz House
10. The East Point Manor
11. The Siegrist-Lonz Farm and Winery
12. The Charles Schneider House
13. The Bretz Winery
14. The Middle Bass Club

N

SCALE
3/4" = 2,000'

TOUR SEVEN
Wine and Peace

(7.9 MILES)

The history of Middle Bass Island mirrors that of South Bass. Both had almost identical beginnings with Alfred Pierpont Edwards selling the land to José de Rivera. The latter owned Middle Bass until the late 1850s when he sold the island, except for the eastern point, to three German immigrants—Andrew Wehrle, William Rehberg, and Joseph Miller (Mueller in German)—and to George Caldwell of New Hampshire. The island had already been logged by its previous owners, who had sold the wood for steamboat fuel, and these four new settlers established vineyards on the cleared land. In 1863, the eastern section of the island was sold by de Rivera to John Lutz (or Lutes), who also planted grapes. Today, Middle Bass Island is noted for its tranquillity and for its wineries. The island architecture reflects a mixture of designs unlike any of those found on the other islands, and residences range from simple farmhouses, to clusters of ornate cottages, to a Frank Lloyd Wright-inspired mansion.

1. The Lonz Winery. Our Middle Bass tour begins at the southern tip of the island, just west of the ferry docks, at the Lonz Winery. The present structure is built on top of the hewn-limestone wine cellar established about 1870 by island pioneer Andrew Wehrle. Wehrle's company, the Golden Eagle Winery, once claimed to be the largest producer of wine in the nation. The original vaulted Golden Eagle cellars are still used by the Lonz Winery; entered through a massive round-arched entrance, the ancient cellar is open for public tours. In 1871 Wehrle built a huge frame pavilion above his winery; it burned in 1923, along with an adjacent hotel that had been built in 1906 when the winery was operated by August Schmidt. Most of the buildings surrounding the winery were built by Wehrle to house workers.

Golden Eagle Wine Cellars, 1874. The Lonz Winery (pictured below) now occupies this site.

The present building was constructed by George F. Lonz, who merged the wine-making enterprises of his father Peter with the Wehrle-Schmidt operations and founded the Lonz Winery. The public wine-tasting rooms and production areas, as well as the structure's castlelike exterior, are the result of the creative imaginations of George Lonz and his builder, Henry Blocker. The winery's unique tower once served as a Lonz family observatory. George Lonz died in 1968. But Meier's Wine Cellars, the current owner, has begun a complete restoration that includes a replanting of the vineyards. Paramount Distilleries, based in Cleveland, purchased Meier's Wine Cellars, based in Cincinnati, in 1976 and

The Lonz Winery

Lonz Winery, based on the islands, in 1981. Lonz Winery is open from 11 A.M. to 10 P.M. from Memorial Day to Labor Day, then on weekends through September. Other island-area wineries owned by Paramount Distilleries include Firelands Wine Cellars, Sandusky, and Mon Ami Wine Cellars, Catawba Island.

Wine cellars at the Lonz Winery

Interior view of restaurant/bar at the Lonz Winery

The Schmidt House

2. The August Schmidt House. Located just east of the Lonz Winery is the residence built by August Schmidt about 1906. It became the home of George F. Lonz in 1926; he lived here until his death in 1968. The building is a late Queen Anne dwelling and features a broad porch, a corner tower, and a Shingle Style roofline.

3. The Middle Bass School. Following Fox Road north to Runkle Road, we see at the very center of the island the Middle Bass School, Town Hall, and cemetery. The one-room schoolhouse, one of only a few in the state still in use as an elementary school, is an excellent example of the Gothic Revival style mixed with Eastlake elements. The cupola and weathervane that top the roof make this an easily identifiable island landmark; the steep gable's decorative woodwork is a testament to the skill of its Victorian-era carpenters.

4. The Middle Bass Town Hall. Across Runkle Road is the building that was constructed by South Bass contractor George Gascoyne in 1877 for $1,875. Now minus its wooden cupola, the Town Hall remains the center of Middle Bass's community activities. With its long windows and decorative window moldings, the structure is another adaptation of Italianate architecture.

The Middle Bass Town Hall

5. The Middle Bass Cemetery. Directly behind the schoolhouse is the cemetery that has served the island more than one hundred years. Many ornate stone monuments may be seen here. Especially worth noting is the elaborate stone-carved Gothic mausoleum of German vintner and island pioneer William Rehberg.

6. The Heise Farmhouse. Across Fox Road from the Middle Bass School and Town Hall is the farmhouse constructed about 1860 for the Schleuse family. Greek Revival and L-shaped in design, it still looks much the same as it did when it was constructed over one hundred twenty years ago.

The Heise Farmhouse

The Gemelch House

7. The Gemelch House. At the end of Fox Road is one of the few brick homes seen in the islands. Anton Fisher, another German vintner, erected this remote island residence after purchasing the land from pioneer George Caldwell in 1874. The home is a fine example of Italianate architecture, with its bracketed cornices and stone door and window moldings. It also sported a decorative front porch that fell into decay and was removed during a recent renovation.

8. The George High House. Directly across Fox Road stands a frame dwelling that is similar in proportions to the brick Gemelch House. This was the home of grape growers George and Anna High, who arrived at Middle Bass in 1870. The Greek Revival structure features a doorway flanked by sidelights, and the home has typical multipaned Greek Revival windows that are framed by their original shutters.

9. The John Lutz House (also known as the Erie House). Heading back along Fox Road, we turn left at Deist Road and follow it to secluded East Point, the area settled by the grape-growing Lutz (or Lutes) family. With its shorefront location, the Lutz House commands an outstanding view of the lake. The dwelling was built about 1863 and is of Italianate design with narrow windows and decorative roof brackets. Several of the homes surrounding this one were built for the Lutz children as they married.

10. The East Point Manor. At the very tip of East Point, this rambling modern stone residence was built about 1925 and modeled after designs made famous by contemporary Chicago architect Frank Lloyd Wright. The unique home was a summer retreat for Harry F. Payer, a prominent Cleveland attorney who later served as assistant U.S. secretary of state. Payer's hundred-acre estate included a golf course, stables, an air strip, and a game preserve. The former stables and wrought-iron fencing that served as entrance gates can be seen near the approach to the manor.

11. The Siegrist-Lonz Farm and Winery. We return to the intersection of Fox and Runkle Roads, where the Middle Bass School and Town Hall stand, and head east on Runkle Road, stopping at the first cluster of buildings on the south side. The simple, frame farmhouse was built about 1866 by vintner John Siegrist. In 1893, he passed the property to his daughter Cora, who was the wife of Peter Lonz, father of George Lonz and founder of the Lonz Winery. Thus this farm was the original Lonz wine-making operation; its unusual square brick wine press stands behind the main house. Today the farm is owned by Meier's Wine Cellars, which plans to renovate the buildings.

The Lutz House

12. The Charles Schneider House. Across from the Siegrist-Lonz farm is the homestead of yet another early islander, Charles Schneider. The dwelling was built about 1870 and served as the Middle Bass Post Office when Schneider's daughter-in-law Thelma lived here. The stylish brackets supporting the eaves identify the style as Italianate.

13. The Bretz Winery. After traveling farther east on Runkle Road and passing the former Bretz family homesteads, we turn north on a winding road and travel through a densely shaded thicket. Near the end of this road stands the winery founded in 1867 by German pioneer Joseph Mueller, one of the original vintners who purchased Middle Bass land from de Rivera. Mueller's grandson, Leslie Bretz, continued wine making in this century until his death in 1985; now his sons operate the winery and produce six kinds of still wines and three sparkling champagnes. The winery is an interesting combination of old and new buildings; its older structures include a board-and-batten press house among their architectural designs. It has not been open to the public since the death of Mr. Bretz.

14. The Middle Bass Club. Backtracking along Runkle, we head north on Fox Road, then west on Lonz Road until it ends. Here, lining two rustic lanes called Grape and Grove avenues, the re-

East Point Manor

markable collection of summer cottages known as the Middle Bass Club is seen. The club was founded in 1874 by a number of influential Toledo businessmen; what began as a private vacation community developed into an exclusive summer resort for the social elite of Toledo, Louisville, Columbus, and Dayton. Island pioneer William Rehberg began selling land to the city dwellers in 1874. By 1876, there were seven cottages and a club house; by 1880, there were twenty cottages and more than two hundred members. In 1882, a new club house was built, designed by Toledo architect E. O. Fallis, who also designed South Bass's monumental Hotel Victory. None of the cottages had kitchens, as meals were taken in the breezy club house. By 1894, the Middle Bass Club included a long dock, boat and bath houses, a laundry, a waterworks, a chapel, and an ice house. The three-story club house was of Eastlake architectural style and stood near the point's southern shore, between Grove Avenue and Lake Erie. Members of the club boasted that four American presidents—Benjamin Harrison, Grover Cleveland, Rutherford B. Hayes, and William Howard Taft—were guests there during their terms in office.

The club house was demolished in 1949, and fire has destroyed some of the cottages over the years, but the resort community in its tranquil, parklike setting still features many fascinating examples of cottage architecture. Included here are Italianate, Gothic, Eastlake, Queen Anne, and Shingle designs, although the mansard roof and dormers of the Second French

George Bretz in front of the Bretz Winery

Empire style dominate the group. Of particular interest are the following three buildings:

A. The Queen Anne-style cottage at the north end of Grape Avenue. Noted for its bulbous porch posts, this structure is likely the work of E. O. Fallis, the designer of the Middle Bass Club and the Hotel Victory.

B. The "Doll House"-type cottage at the end of Grove Avenue. This dwelling combines Second French Empire and Italianate styles; it was built about 1880.

C. The Second French Empire cottage facing Grove Avenue. It features an interesting mansard roof, wide wrap-around verandas, and rounded wall dormer windows.

Grape Avenue, 1895

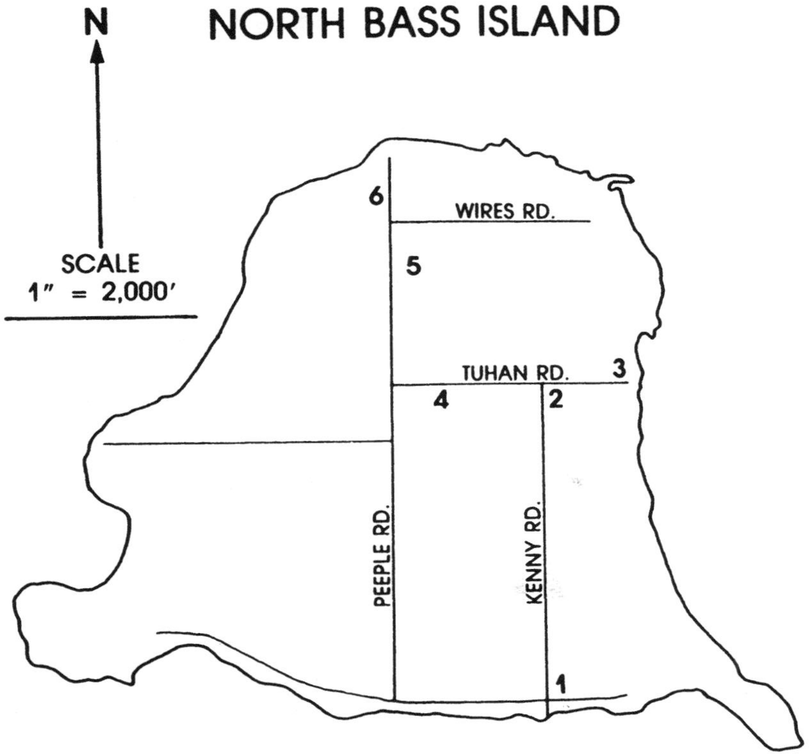

TOUR 8
Remote Tranquility
(1.7 miles)

1. The Wine Cellar
2. The Smith House
3. The Simon Fox Farmhouse
4. The Isle of Saint George
   Congregational Church
5. The George Wires House
6. The Snide-Seefield House

NORTH BASS ISLAND

N

SCALE
1" = 2,000'

WIRES RD.

TUHAN RD.

KENNY RD.

PEEPLE RD.

TOUR EIGHT
Remote Tranquillity

(1.7 MILES)

Only a few miles from the Canadian border, North Bass Island (also called Isle Saint George) was settled by Simon and Peter Fox. These two brothers arrived in 1850, cleared timber, planted vineyards, and established wine cellars. Unlike South and Middle Bass, North Bass was never touched by commercial and resort development and to this day remains more or less a huge vineyard. Only four improved-surface roads cross the island, and the buildings located along these are mostly of Greek Revival or Italianate design, with residences built on a T- or L-shaped plan. Most have limestone rubble foundations. Farm buildings, a church, a twine house, and a few other outbuildings are the only structures located here. All of North Bass is owned by Meier's Wine Cellars, which also owns the Lonz Winery and the Siegrist-Lonz Farm seen at Middle Bass. Permission should be obtained from the winery's local manager before touring the area.

1. The Wine Cellar. Our tour begins at the southern end of Kenny Road. Here we see a pavilion-like structure with a foundation of native limestone. Since the stone lower level is similar to many other wine cellars on the islands, the property likely was the site of a wine cellar. The pavilion is newer than the foundation, but little is known of the history of this building.

2. The Smith House. At the northern end of Kenny, where it meets Tuhan Road, stands an L-shaped farmhouse built about 1865. Otherwise a typical island farm dwelling, it is somewhat unusual because of the circular vent in its front gable and its simple Italianate porch.

3. The Simon Fox Farmhouse. Heading east on Tuhan, we arrive at the farm of one of the earliest island settlers. Simon Fox

The Fox Farmstead

and his brother Peter bought five hundred acres of land on North Bass in the 1850s and established the wine-making industry on this island. Today this farmstead is the residence of Meier's Wine Cellars' local manager. The house was built about 1860; it is a fine Greek Revival home with the sidelighted doorway and transom typical of its style. The building is also noted for its rare Greek Revival porches. The front porch has fluted Doric columns, and the recessed side porch sports wooden arches. Just northeast of the dwelling, Fox's dock and a two-story twine house are maintained by the present owner.

Fox Farmstead, 1874

The Congregational Church

4. The Isle of Saint George Congregational Church. Backtracking and heading toward the western end of Tuhan Road, we arrive at the most stylistically impressive structure on the island. The land for this church and its adjacent cemetery was donated by island pioneer Roswell Nichols in 1850, and recently the forty residents of North Bass have undertaken the building's restoration. Constructed about 1880, the church features an exotic ogee-arched stained-glass window; here graceful, double-curved molding comes to a point above the colored glass. Other impressive architectural elements include the scalloped shingle front gable with an oculus, or round window, and the large, carved brackets supporting the entrance canopy. The delicate, off-center open-air belfry particularly is worth noting.

5. The George Wires House. From Tuhan, we turn on to Peeple Road and follow it north nearly to Wires Road. Here is the large home of George Wires. Wires was forty years old when he arrived at North Bass and established a thriving orchard on the island. He later married Susan Fox, a member of the pioneering Fox family.

The couple raised ten children on the island, some of whom remained at this family homestead into the twentieth century. The Wires residence is a large Greek Revival variation of the typical L-shaped farmhouse plan. It was built between 1850 and 1860.

6. The Snide-Seefield House. On the west side of Peeple, north of Wires and set well back from the road, stands the home of J. Snide. Snide established orchards and vineyards on the island before 1874. His former residence is a farmhouse variation of the Gothic Revival architectural style.

Steamships
THE LINK TO THE MAINLAND

Most of the steamships that once traveled the waters between the Bass Islands and the mainland are gone forever. Some were dismantled, some burned, some wrecked, some run aground, some converted into barges or tugs, and some sold for scrap. For many of these mighty vessels, all that remain are photographs taken at the height—or the depth—of the ship's career.

The pages that follow are designed to give the reader a glimpse of the great era of Bass Island steamship travel by providing first an introductory summary of that era and then a more detailed look at the history of the island steamship trade including photographs of some of the steamships that once navigated the waters around the Bass Islands.

Introduction

For the inhabitants of the Bass Islands, water transportation has always been a vital concern. Prior to the mid-1850s, the earliest islanders used small sailing vessels to carry themselves, their supplies, and their export products to and from the mainland. In addition, wood-burning steamers occasionally would stop at the islands to refuel, using timber from the abundant forests, and would pick up goods or passengers during these stopovers. But in the early 1860s, when numerous German grape-growers began to settle the islands and the wine trade grew, regular steamship service became profitable. And, as access to the islands increased, so did the number of tourists who came to enjoy the pleasant scenery and peaceful atmosphere that the region offered.

The Bass Islands became more and more popular as a resort area, and the number of steamship routes and the frequency of travel along them steadily grew. For islanders and others who

Several steamers gather at Put-in-Bay in July 1869 to embark veterans attending the Grand Army of the Republic convention. The vessels are *(from left to right)* the *R. N. Rice,* the *Lake Breeze,* the *Evening Star,* the *Reindeer,* and the *Jay Cooke.* Gibraltar Island forms the backdrop

regularly made trips between the Bass Islands and the mainland, the names of specific ships were household words and their routes and schedules were known by heart. The most heavily traveled steamship route ran straight from Sandusky (which featured rail service going directly to the main ship docks) to the islands. This run often included stops on the Marblehead Peninsula and Kelleys Island. Another important route stopped at the Bass Islands on the way from Sandusky to Detroit. Occasional service also was offered between both Toledo and Cleveland and the islands. A shorter, more local route existed between the islands and the region that included Port Clinton, Catawba, Lakeside, and Marblehead.

Travel was most frequent in the summer, when thousands of resort visitors crowded the ships; interspersed with the regularly scheduled trips were weekend and holiday excursions and moonlight cruises. In the spring, steamship service was also important, for it enabled the islanders to replenish supplies and catch up with mainland business that had been neglected during the forced isolation of the winter months when the lake was frozen. Autumn was harvest time, and in the fall vessels carried grapes—sometimes as many as 1,600 barrels of them—as well as peaches, wine, and other island products to Detroit, Toledo, Port Clinton, Catawba, and Sandusky.

The heyday of steamship service to the Bass Islands lasted from the 1870s through the turn of the century. During the first decade or so of the 1900s, however, the popularity of moving pictures

The Fox wharf at Put-in-Bay is shown in this turn-of-the-century photo. The vessels are (*from left to right*) the *State of New York*, the steam yacht *Falcon*, and the *City of the Straits*

made folks more likely to spend weekends in their hometowns, and the advent of the automobile made close-to-home travel easier and more fun. Both of these turn-of-the-century inventions contributed greatly to a decline in travel to the Bass Islands. By the beginning of World War I, much of the lake traffic between the islands and the mainland had ceased, and daily service from Toledo, Sandusky, and Detroit was all that remained. After the war, Prohibition, which destroyed the island wine industry, and the Depression, which further damaged the region's economy, dealt the final blows ending the great era of the island steamships. A few steam vessels continued to make runs to the islands until 1948, when the *Put-in-Bay*, the last steamer, made its final voyage from Detroit to Sandusky.

The *Put-in-Bay*

A History of the Island Steamship Trade

In 1846 Daniel Dibble, a Sandusky shipwright, was hired by Ira and Datus Kelley and others to build a steamboat on Kelleys Island. The resulting vessel, the *Islander,* ran on a varying schedule for the next eight years and called at Kelleys Island, Marblehead, Sandusky, Venice, Ottawa City, and Fremont. In the spring of 1854—the same year that José de Rivera came to the Bass Islands and settlement of the region began in earnest—the great era of island steamship travel began when the *Islander's* schedule was changed to include a stop at Put-in-Bay. The *Islander* was the first of nearly half a hundred ships that island residents and visitors would come to know during the next several decades.

The Kelley family became increasingly aware of the financial advantages of operating ships in the Bass Islands area. In 1855, the Kelleys added the *Island Queen* to their line. And in 1866, the *Evening Star* was purchased by the family from its owners in Saginaw, Michigan.

Meanwhile, Peter and Simon Fox, who had settled at North Bass Island in 1859, decided that they too would take part in the steamship trade. In 1863, they invested in the business by tying in with a Detroit man named Walter Ashley, and together they operated the *Philo Parsons* between Sandusky and Detroit, with the

The *Evening Star*

Put-in-Bay in the early 1890s with the steamers (*from left to right*)
City of Sandusky, Chief Justice Waite, and *Pearl*

Bass Islands as a stopping-off point. In 1867, the Fox family
bought their own steamer, the *Eighth Ohio*. They placed her on
nearly the same route used by the Kelley ships. Business
improved, and two years later they bought a larger vessel, the
Reindeer.

Competition between the Fox and Kelley interests became
fierce, and much haggling went on during the winter of 1869-70,
ending in a merger which formed the Lake Erie Steamboat Company, with Alfred Kelley as president. The *Reindeer* was placed on
the route between the Bass Islands and Toledo, while the *Evening
Star* continued to travel from the islands to Sandusky. By 1873,
the Kelley-Fox company was experiencing other competition on
the Sandusky route; to make things worse, both the *Reindeer* and
the *Evening Star* needed major overhauls. The fierce competition
and the high cost of upkeep expenses resulted in the disbanding of
the company. The *Reindeer* and *Evening Star* were sold to
parties in Toledo and Detroit, respectively.

Much of the competition that had threatened and helped to
destroy Alfred Kelley's company had come from John P. Clark, a
dry dock and vessel owner from Detroit. Along with Selah and
Ollie Dustin and Walter Ashley (who had operated the *Philo
Parsons* with the Fox family), Clark was involved in steamboat
trade from Detroit to Sandusky via the Bass Islands; indeed, the
Dustin-Ashley-Clark sidewheeler *Dart* had made regular runs along
this route as early as 1862. The *Dart* and *Philo Parsons* were
followed by a succession of steamships, such as the *Jay Cooke,*

The *Frank E. Kirby*

the *Gazelle,* the *Riverside,* the *Pearl,* and the beautiful sidewheeler *Alaska.* These ships traveled the Sandusky-Bass Islands-Detroit route until around 1890.

When Clark died in 1880, Walter Ashley, working closely with Clark's estate, became manager of Clark's steamship line. A decade later, the Ashley and Dustin Line was formed with the building of the *Frank E. Kirby.* This ship, nicknamed the "Flyer of

The *Chief Justice Waite*

The *Arrow*

the Lakes," was one of the best known vessels on the Sandusky-Bass Islands-Detroit route, which she followed from 1890 to 1922. Beginning in 1873 with the steamer *Gazelle*, the Clark interests also covered the route from the islands to Cleveland. (They were preceded here only by the *Messenger* in 1866 and by the sidewheeler *Lotta Bernard* in 1870.) In addition, the Clark line also ran the sidewheel steamers *Pearl* and *Alaska* (both of which had serviced the Detroit-Sandusky run) between Cleveland and the Bass Islands. Buffalo was added to the route in 1878, but the run proved unprofitable and was dropped.

In Toledo, meanwhile, under the leadership of Charles West, yet another steamship company had formed in 1873. Under the name of the Toledo, Lake Erie, and Island Steamboat Company, West and his associates had bought the *Reindeer* from the Fox-Kelley line when the two families bowed out of the steamship trade rather than renovate the ship. The next year, West's company brought out the elegant sidewheel steamer *Chief Justice Waite*, powered by the *Reindeer's* engine. The *Waite* ran between Toledo and the Bass Islands from 1874 until 1888, when she was sold to a Chicago company. Other ships that plied the route between Toledo and the Bass Islands were the *Gazelle*, the *Pearl*, the *Metropolis*, the *Grace McMillan*, and the *Leila*.

Another important name in the history of the Bass Islands

A rare interior view of the *Chippewa* in the 1920s. One can imagine the jazz music of the period coming from the bandstand at the left. The ornate woodwork and the rugs and wicker furniture are worth noticing; the ship's dining salon can be seen through the glass doors

steamship trade was that of island settler Andrew Wehrle. Wehrle, a German wine grower and founder of Middle Bass Island's enormous Golden Eagle Winery, brought out the small propeller ship *Golden Eagle* in 1872; this was replaced by the small passenger steamer *American Eagle* in 1880. Two years later, the Sandusky and Island Steamboat Company was established with Wehrle as president. Wehrle's namesake ship, the *A. Wehrle, Jr.,* was built in 1891 but she ran for only a short time between the islands and the mainland. Four years later the company brought out the popular passenger steamer *Arrow,* which was powered by the *Jay Cooke*'s engine. When the *Arrow* burned in 1922, she was replaced by the equally popular *Chippewa.* Together with Ashley and Dustin's *Frank E. Kirby,* the *Arrow* and the *Chippewa* are perhaps the best remembered of the island passenger steamers.

In 1890, the Detroit and Cleveland Steam Navigation Company put the sidewheeler *City of the Straits* on the Cleveland to Put-in-Bay and Toledo route. Six years later, through a cooperative arrangement with the Cleveland and Buffalo Transit Company (known as C & B), the *State of New York* began making the same run. This service continued until 1914 with only slight variations. Another C & B steamer, the *State of Ohio,* was later to be a familiar sight on this route until 1917. C & B operated regular week-

The *State of Ohio*

day Cleveland to Put-in-Bay service with the *City of Erie* from 1914 to 1926, and with the appealingly named *Goodtime* from 1925 to 1938. A final cruise ship, the well-known *Alabama*, made the last weekday excursion to the islands from Cleveland in 1945.

The forties saw the end of Bass Island steamship travel. The *Erie Isle* ran as an auto ferry between Catawba and Put-in-Bay from 1930 until 1946 but later ended up as a lowly coal barge. The island harbor namesake *Put-in-Bay*, the last of the true island steamers, made a final voyage from Detroit to Sandusky in 1948.

The *Goodtime*

The *Mystic Isle*

Of course other ships, such as the motor vessel *Mystic Isle,* have continued over the years to travel to and from the Bass Islands. The Burger Boat Company of Manitowoc, Wisconsin, built *Mystic Isle* for the Erie Isle Ferry Company in 1942. Today the ships seen in the region are diesel propelled, and their silhouettes differ radically from those of the great steamers, like the lovely *B. F. Ferris,* with their elegant sidewheels and tall smokestacks. The names of the great steamboat skippers—George and Victor Brown, Harry Tyrie, Ed McNelly, and Frank Hamilton (who was the last skipper of the *Put-in-Bay* and later became a respected historian of Great Lakes shipping)—are nearly forgotten now, as are the vessels they captained.

Today's ships are faster and more efficient than their predecessors, and a boat trip from Port Clinton or Catawba to the islands is still an exciting experience for the Bass visitor. But as the modern tourist ship approaches or leaves Put-in-Bay, her passengers may wish to close their eyes for a moment and visualize the great steamships that provided a mainland link and helped create the history of the Bass Islands.

Glossary of
Architectural Terms

Batten ('bat-en). A usually thin, narrow strip of wood used to seal or reinforce the vertical joint between two boards.

Captain's walk (from its use by sea captains during their absence from the sea; also called widow's walk, from its similar use by their wives). A railed observation deck atop a waterfront house.

Cornice ('kor-nis). The projecting horizontal part of a roof which extends beyond the wall.

Cresting. A decorative ridge on a roof, usually as a continuous series of ornaments. A crest is the single ornament; cresting is the continuous feature.

Cupola ('kyu-po-la). A small structure, square, octagonal, or round, built upon a roof.

Dentil ('den-til) **board-and-batten.** Small rectangular batten intended for ornamental effect by alternation of light and shadow.

Double-hung windows (also called vertical slide windows). A type of window having two balanced sashes that operate vertically.

Fretwork. Decoration consisting of intricate, interlaced openwork of wood, metal, or stone, usually in relief.

Gable. The triangular piece of wall under the ridge of a pitched roof.

Gingerbread (from the lavish gilding often applied to the cake of the same name). Any superfluous ornament in architecture.

Gothic arch. An arch that forms a point, rather than a curve, at the apex.

Mansard ('man-sard) **roof.** A roof having two slopes on all sides, the lower of which is steeper than the upper one.

Molding. Any strip of material used for ornamentation, covering joints, or concealing wires.

Ogee ('o-jee) **arch** (also called keel arch). A pointed arch, slightly convex near the apex.

Parapet ('par-a-pet). A low wall or railing at the edge of a roof, terrace, or balcony.

Scroll. A spiral or scroll-shaped band, usually in relief, to contain an inscription.

Sidelights. A pair of narrow windows flanking a door.

Transom ('tran-som) **window.** A hinged window over a door usually for ventilation.

Glossary of Architectural Styles

American architecture is unique, and the architecture of the Bass Islands is an excellent example of that uniqueness. The designs seen in American architecture are often difficult to categorize. Many structures are catalog or handbook variations of standard architectural styles constructed by local builders or by traveling carpenters and masons. Other buildings are products of a blending of styles or of the transitions from one style to another. And of course each community or region contains a few really spectacular creations that epitomize particular styles and are the work of talented architects.

The Bass Islands offer a delightful cornucopia of architectural styles, ranging from elegant summer residences of the rich to simple dwellings of local farmers. This glossary is intended to help the tourist identify and appreciate island architecture.

Bass Island Styles

Greek Revival (1840-75). This style is exemplified by simple, rectangular, frame houses with offset doorways surrounded by sidelights or transoms or both. Roofs are low pitched; windows are flat topped and double hung. The plans often feature a two-story main section with a one-story wing attached (called the "upright-with-wing" plan). Generally these structures have wide eaves and no porches.

Gothic Revival (1850-1900). Dominated by the steep, pointed arches of rooflines, windows, and moldings, Gothic buildings may be of brick, stone, or frame construction. They feature heavily carved gable moldings (gingerbread), decorative porches, and vertical battens covering wood siding joints (the "board-and-batten" style).

Romanesque Revival (1860-1900). The Romanesque style is often found on churches, mausoleums, or public buildings made of brick or stone. It is dominated by round-arched openings and often is incorporated into other styles of architecture.

Italianate (1865-80). This design, seen very often on the Bass Islands, features ornate decorations such as brackets supporting roof cornices, decorative window and door moldings, carved porch woodwork, tall, narrow windows, and bay windows. Building plans may be square, rectangular, or L-shaped.

Italian Villa (1865-80). This design is similar to Italianate and is often characterized by a corner tower, wooden or iron cresting (railings) at the roofline, and a large, wrap-around porch.

Second French Empire (1870-80). This design is also similar to Italianate but is dominated by a sloping mansard roof above the main part of the house, with dormer windows piercing this roof. Buildings of this style are frequently squarish and small in scale with wide porches.

Stick Style (1880-99). This type of architecture is less ornate than other styles; it is characterized by boards in vertical, diagonal, and horizontal patterns applied to the walls or to projecting gables. These buildings are of frame construction.

Queen Anne (1885-1905). The Queen Anne style is often called "Victorian." Its buildings are irregular in plan, and a variety of construction and decorative materials (such as bricks, shingles, clapboard, stone or wooden moldings, leaded and stained glass) may be used on a single structure. The style is often dominated by a rounded corner tower and features high roofs in many shapes, gingerbreaded wrap-around porches, decorative chimneys, and decorative (often geometric) window and gable designs.

Eastlake (1890-1900). This style is sometimes referred to as "Steamboat Gothic." Elements include furniturelike woodwork (such as knobs and spindles) produced on lathes. Other features are those of Stick Style or Queen Anne architecture.

Shingle Style (1890-1910). This style takes its name from its wooden shingle-covered walls. Elaborate examples are usually irregular in plan, whereas less elaborate versions are often more symmetrical. Buildings of this design generally are simpler in overall execution than those of other styles.

Colonial Revival (1890-1930). These structures may be symmetrical or asymmetrical and usually have simple, formal, rectangular floor plans. Features include classical motifs (such as dentil moldings, Corinthian capitals, or Roman columns), oval or semi-oval openings, and windows and doors that are generally flat topped with geometric mullions. They are usually of frame construction.

Index of Buildings by Architectural Styles

(Listed by Tour Stopping Point)

Greek Revival

The Kite Shop, *1-10*
The Acorn Club, *3-4*
The Ruh House, *3-5*
The Philip Vroman House, *4-8*
The José de Rivera Estate, *4-11*
The Heise Farmhouse, *7-6*
The George High House, *7-8*
The Simon Fox Farmhouse, *8-3*
The George Wires House, *8-5*

Gothic Revival

The Carriage House, *1-2*
Saint Paul's Epis-
   copal Church, *1-17*
The Reibel House Hotel, *4-5*
The Daniel Vroman House, *4-7*
The Cooke Castle, *6-2*
The Middle Bass School, *7-3*
The Middle Bass Cemetery, *7-5*
The Snide-Seefield House, *8-6*

Romanesque Revival

Mother of Sorrows
   Catholic Church, *1-18*
The Crown Hill Cemetery, *5-6*

Italianate

The Crescent Tavern, *1-4*
The Country House, *1-7*
The Kite Shop, *1-10*
Idlor House, *1-19*
Ted's Tackle Shop, *1-20*
The Crew's Nest, *1-24*
The Dodge House, *1-25*
The Acorn Club, *3-4*
The Ruh House, *3-5*
The Henry Burggraf Farm, *3-6*
The Engel Farm, *4-1*
The Alois Niele House, *4-3*
The George Bickford House, *4-4*
The Philip Vroman House, *4-8*
The Charles Miller House, *4-14*
The van Dohren Farmhouse, *5-5*
The Middle Bass Town Hall, *7-4*
The Gemelch House, *7-7*
The John Lutz House, *7-9*
The Charles Schneider
   House, *7-12*
The "Doll House"–type
   Cottage, *7-14*
The Smith House, *8-2*

Index of Sites

(Listed by Tour Stopping Point)

Tour 1: Vintage Village
1. Island Park (De Rivera Park)
2. Carriage House
3. Schlitz Ice House
4. Crescent Tavern
5. Round House
6. Park Hotel
7. Country House
8. Frosty's
9. The Colonial
10. The Kite Shop
11. Heritage Antiques/ The Lone Willow
12. Town Hall
13. The Blacksmith Shop
14. Tony's Place
15. Put-in-Bay School
16. Gascoyne House
17. Saint Paul's Episcopal Church
18. Mother of Sorrows Catholic Church
19. Idlor House
20. Ted's Tackle Shop
21. Wharf Side
22. Doller Colonial House
23. Doller Villa
24. Crew's Nest
25. Dodge House
26. Put-in-Bay Yacht Club
27. Warren Cottage

Tour 2: Science and Serenity
1. Bayview House
2. Stone Laboratory Research Station
3. The State Fish Hatchery
4. Feick Cottage

Tour 3: In the Shadow of Perry's Monument
1. Perry's Victory and International Peace Memorial
2. The Hunker Villa
3. Inselruhe
4. Acorn Club
5. Ruh House
6. Henry Burggraf Farm
7. Matthias Burggraf Farm

Tour 4: Vineyards and Vikings
1. Engel Farm
2. The Stone Wine Press
3. Alois Niele House (Wiesler House)
4. George Bickford House
5. Reibel House Hotel
6. Foster Farm
7. Daniel Vroman House
8. Philip Vroman House
9. Cooper's Restaurant
10. Mortimer Wine Press

◆